THE BUSINESS PLAN GUIDE

From the

FAST-TRACK BUSINESS EXPERT SERIES OF BOOKS AND COURSES

Mark A. Philip
2012

THE BUSINESS PLAN GUIDE

From the
FAST-TRACK BUSINESS EXPERT SERIES
OF BOOKS AND COURSES

BY MARK A. PHILIP

A Management Guide To Developing A Persuasive Business Plan

The Business Plan Guide provides a step-by-step management guide of how to prepare and author a persuasive business plan, which can be used to attract investors to your business or simply guide your business through the myriad challenges you will face.

Acknowledgements and Thanks

Special thanks to my wife, Jean, for putting up with all my idiosyncrasies and the time I have spent preparing my books rather than participating in other activities. Thanks to my daughters, Elaine, Abigail and Zoe for buying my first books and reading through the first drafts.

A big thank you to my editor, Peter Rock, for all his hard work reading and correcting my work and who diligently supported me in this effort, always with a kind word to go along with his suggestions.

Table of Contents

HOW TO WRITE A PERSUASIVE BUSINESS PLAN

INTRODUCTION

A good business plan should clearly define a company's products or services, lay out how the business intends to operate, in which markets it will operate, and how it intends to generate sales and profits from its well-defined client or customer base. The level of detail in a business plan very much depends on how you intend to use it; whether as a personal guide to running your business or to convince others to make an investment or partner with you in some way, or a dozen other possible uses. If it is just for personal use, then it may not need to be too detailed, but if you intend to use it to gain investments in your business, then you need it to be robust enough to stand up to scrutiny from the investors you approach.

I have written this guide to be used by business executives, MBA students and graduates who are part of an established business, but also for entrepreneurs and business owners who own a small business or new start-up. If you need a short business plan as a guide to develop your company then try the "One-Page Business Plan For Busy Entrepreneurs" (see page 10). By answering a few short questions, you can quickly formulate a plan to guide you through the next phase of your business.

If on the other hand, you need a detailed business plan to attract investors, you should follow the Detailed Business Plan Guide (see page 14), which will walk you through how to construct a comprehensive business plan capable of attracting significant investment. I ask a lot of questions of you and your business, so you may need to approach this one section at a time, and take a break in between writing each section. You should also leave the writing of the first section, the Executive Summary, until you have finished all the other parts of the plan. This will allow you to create the best summary for your Business Plan.

The Essence of a Great Business Plan

The most important part of the business plan is the process of creating it, which forces you to think about strategic, operational, tactical, human and financial aspects of how your business will work. It will require research and investigation with regard to your customers, markets, and competition; it will require you to be creative in thinking through what it is you are offering and why someone should choose your product or service over those offered by others. You need to figure out how to reach your customers, with what type of message and which channel or media to use, how your product will be made and shipped or where a service will be provided, how you will ensure the quality of your product and to ensure you are meeting your customer's needs. And, it will require you to forecast sales and expenses and how and when you might make a profit or at least have enough cash to continue to grow your business. Finally, it should also convince a potential investor that your business would be a great investment and provide them with a good return.

Scrutinize your assumptions

If you have done your homework properly, then the business plan should be able to stand up to fairly rigorous scrutiny, but be prepared to answer a few questions. What assumptions have you made and why? What market research have you done? How will you compete against a particular competitor? Be prepared to discuss what you would do if your assumptions turn out to be wrong or that the market changes in some way. So let's get started; either choose to go with the One Page Business Plan for Busy Entrepreneurs (see page 10), or the Detailed Business Plan (see page 14).

For the Entrepreneur or Small Business Looking For A Day-To-Day Plan.

If you do not intend to use your business plan to raise capital for the business, but rather just to use it as a guidance document for you to develop your business, you can be less rigorous with the analysis but you will still need to think carefully. After following the One-Page

Business Plan instructions, you may still want to read the Detailed Business Plan outline provided, as it may give you additional ideas you want to think about in relation to developing your business further. For those of you who just want a quick fix to their strategy, the One-Page Business Plan For Busy Entrepreneurs may be the way to go.

For The Money Raising Detailed Business Plan

You will find the outline of the key ingredients of your business plan followed by a detailed description of each section, after the One Page Business Plan for Busy Entrepreneurs.

THE ONE-PAGE BUSINESS PLAN FOR BUSY ENTREPRENEURS

If you plan to use your business plan as a guidance document for your new or evolving business, you can be less rigorous with the analysis but you will still need to think carefully. You may still want to follow the detailed outline provided, as it may give you some ideas about how to further develop your business and explore other opportunities. Below I will provide you a guideline followed by a one-page template you can use for your business.

ONE PAGE GUIDELINE

Your Business Mission

What is the mission or vision you have for your business? What do you want your company to do for your customers?

The Problem or Need

Define the business problem or unmet need you have identified.

The Business Solution/Competitive Advantage.

Provide a brief statement of your solution to the business problem or unmet need. What is your competitive advantage?

The Business Opportunity/Market Size/Competition

Define the business opportunity scope and market size. How large is this opportunity (use numbers where possible, such as customers, or potential sales)? Is the market growing? Who are your key competitors, their strengths and weaknesses and how can you beat them?

Marketing Goals

Define your top 4 or 5 marketing goals for the next year (or two). What do you want to achieve in terms of sales, new customers, profitability, cash flow, penetration of the market, market share, etc.?

Marketing Strategies

Define the marketing strategies you intend to employ to achieve your business goal and estimate the cost of the activities involved. Include your advertising and promotional activities as well as any specific sales and distributor activities. For example, you may intend to advertise in the local paper or on LinkedIn, email past customers, or run a special promotion.

Other Expenses

Include an estimate of all your other expenses: people costs, facilities, utilities, Internet access, phone, travel, product costs, distribution costs, legal costs, research and development costs and general and administrative costs.

Financial Projections

Think through the sales you anticipate from your marketing strategies and estimate the revenue for each month. Then calculate your expenses. This should allow you to calculate how much cash is left over each month or your monthly profits. If you are feeling ambitious, add year two and three!

THE ONE PAGE BUSINESS PLAN TEMPLATE

Company Name:_____ Date: _____
Phone:_____ Website:_____

Business Vision/Mission: _____
_____

Business Problem/Unmet Need: _____
_____

Business Solution/Competitive Advantage: _____
_____
_____

Marketing Goals (be specific/must be measurable):
1. _____
_____
2. _____
_____
3. _____
_____
4. _____
_____
5. _____
_____

Marketing Strategies: Cost ($)
1. _____   _____
_____
2. _____   _____
_____
3. _____   _____
_____
4. _____   _____
_____
5. _____   _____
_____

Other Expenses: Cost ($)
_____   _____
_____   _____
_____   _____
_____   _____
_____   _____

Financial Projection:

Month	1	2	3	4	5	6	7	8	9	10	11	12
Sales												
Expenses												
Profit												

THE DETAILED BUSINESS PLAN GUIDE:
THE OUTLINE

1. Executive Summary
2. Vision, Mission, Strategic Plan
   - Vision
   - Mission
   - Values
   - Strategic Planning SWOT Analysis
   - Business Goals
3. The Industry, The Company, The Product, The Technology
   - The Industry
   - The Company
   - The Product
   - Value Proposition
   - Sustainable Competitive Advantage
   - The Technology
   - Intellectual Property
4. Market Research and Analysis
   - Quantify
   - Market Research
   - The Market
   - The Competition
   - Sales Projections
5. Marketing Plan
   - The Market Plan Role
   - Marketing Goals
   - Pricing
   - Positioning
   - Advertising and Promotion
   - Sales and Distribution
   - Measurement
6. Development Plan
   - Product Development
   - Milestones, Costs & Risks
   - Development Financials
7. Operating Plan
   - Location, Facilities and Improvements
   - Manufacturing plan
   - Labor force

- Distribution
8. Key Personnel
    - Organization & Key Personnel
    - Compensation
    - Board of Directors
9. Finance and Financial Statements
    - Ownership
    - Sources and Uses of Funds
    - Financial Statements
    - Pro Forma Financial Statements
    - Exit Strategies & Valuation
    - Contingency Plans

THE DETAILED BUSINESS PLAN GUIDE:
WALK-THROUGH

1. EXECUTIVE SUMMARY

KEY CONTENT	GUIDANCE
Executive Summary	Write this last. No more than one page. Define your product, the market size, your target customers and their unmet need. Succinctly state the specific benefits customers will experience when they buy your product and how this compares to the competition. Briefly describe what you have achieved to date in development, sales, market share, etc. Define your financial status and plan. If Approaching Investors: • State specifically what you want (how much money) and what it is for. • Define potential exit strategies and values for the investors.

By following the guide above, write a sentence or two on each bullet point to create an executive summary of your business plan. It is definitely best to write this last after you have constructed the detail of the business plan so you can summarize your plan succinctly.

Define the business you are in and the market you will serve, have a clear definition of your product, the target customers, and how your product will benefit those customers. Talk about your competitive advantage, how you intend to develop the market, the type of financial results you expect within a reasonable timeframe, and how the value of the business will evolve.

If you are pitching your business to potential investors, one of the most important aspects to include in your Executive Summary is a rational exit strategy. You have to be able to clearly define how the investor will realize a gain from the money they have invested, not just an increase in value, but also an ability to liquidate their asset.

You also need to include a clear statement of what you are asking for: the amount of funds you intend to raise, and how those funds will be used in the business. Some business plans also include the proportion of ownership you are willing to offer in exchange for the investment, although you may chose to provide this detail at a later stage.

2. VISION, MISSION, STRATEGIC PLAN

KEY CONTENT	ANALYSIS
Vision	What is your vision for the company in terms of growth, values, employees, and contributions to society? What is the ultimate goal of your company? What are you trying to achieve? What should your company stand for?
Mission	What are the key strategies of the company from your customer's perspective? What needs do you want to fulfill? What makes you stand out?
Values	What do you and your company stand for? What is it that is an important part of how you want people to operate and to be perceived?
Strategic Planning SWOT Analysis	Define the strengths and weaknesses of your organization, and the opportunities and threats your company faces from the market place.
Strategic Goals	What are the top 4-5 strategic goals you are pursuing to achieve your mission and vision? What are your goals for the next 3-5 years, but also for the next year and next quarter?

Vision, Mission and Values

Most vision or mission statements used by companies today totally miss the point and are far from visionary or capable of motivating a workforce to accomplish some overarching goal they can all get behind and believe in. Your vision statement should be unshakeable and something everyone in the company can relate to as well as your customers.

By contrast, your mission statement should really reflect your customers' needs and what it is you plan to do to stand out as a company to fulfill those needs. And your value statements should reflect the values you want your company to reflect in all its activities. It is these set of values that will also allow your employees the ability to act appropriately and independently and still portray the image you want of your company, even when you are not present.

The SWOT Analysis and Strategic Imperatives

A useful technique to derive your strategy is known as the SWOT analysis, or Strengths, Weaknesses, Opportunities and Threats analysis. Start by defining as many of your company's strengths and weaknesses as possible and by defining as many as possible market opportunities and threats. It is best to do this initially without restrictions and to ask as many of your key people to contribute as possible. Once you have all the inputs you can start to rank them in order of importance and value and try to condense them down to a workable list. After honing down the list to just the most important 3 or 4 strengths, weaknesses, opportunities and threats, you should then synthesize strategies that make use of the company's strengths and play to the market opportunities. Similarly, you should also formulate strategies that play to your strengths and fend off the market threats you face, strategies that focus on opportunities and help address your weaknesses and, finally, strategies that focus on market threats and help you with your weaknesses. This exercise is critical in helping you create a well-rounded approach to your business.

After defining the best strategies to deal with each of the paired components, you should then rank the most important combination of strategies that will be the focus of your company to help you achieve your vision and mission statements; your so-called strategic imperatives. In selecting the most important strategies, make sure that you haven't overlooked a strategy that could be vital to your survival. You can't do everything of course, and 5 or 6 strategies are usually enough for any company, but don't leave out a strategy that could ensure your survival.

For a more detailed explanation of the process and how best to derive an optimal strategy for your business, you should obtain a copy of my business guidebook: The Strategic Plan Guide, available from Amazon.com and CreateSpace.com.

It is best to complete this section on Vision, Mission and Strategy before you move onto the next section, as it will help you develop the rest of your plan and keep you focused on what is important to your business.

3. THE INDUSTRY, THE COMPANY, THE PRODUCT, THE TECHNOLOGY.

KEY CONTENT	GUIDANCE
The Industry	Describe the industry you are in, the different market segments, historical and projected growth, profit projections, new trends in the industry, key players in the market, major products, new products and technologies that may change the landscape.
The Company	Describe the business area in which your company is in, or will enter, and what it will offer. Define the size of the company, its capabilities, strengths and weaknesses and its key customers. Discuss ownership and structure of the company.
The Product or Service	Describe the product or service to be sold; it's unique features and benefits, the value proposition, your significant advantages over the competition, state of development. Describe any intellectual property: patents, trade secrets or proprietary features. What will enable you to achieve a favorable position in your industry?
The Technology (for technology driven companies)	Describe the technology used, your unique position, state of evolution and any trends or planned development needs. Do you own patents and the freedom to operate?

Preparing your assessment of the industry in which you are in should be straightforward by following the questions in the table. What market segments exist? What has been the historical growth and profitability of the industry? Who are the key players and the major products that dominate the industry, and what do you and others anticipate how the industry may change in the future and why? What are the major influences shaping your industry today and tomorrow?

Defining your company, product and technology should be as realistic as possible; try not to exaggerate. How big is your company? What has been its history? What are your strengths and weaknesses, and what are your core capabilities? Who are your key customers?

How would you describe your key products or services? What are their key strengths and weaknesses? Which specific market segments and needs do they serve? What are your value proposition and your sustainable competitive advantage?

Value Proposition:

One definition of a value proposition is: the unique value your business provides to your customers. In other words, the perceived value created when you meet the so-called unmet need of your target market. More simply, it is the benefit a customer receives when they buy your product or service.

Sustainable Competitive Advantage:

A sustainable competitive advantage is an attribute or group of attributes that allows a company to outperform its competitors and is not easily reproduced, thus creating a long-term benefit.

Technology

List out the technologies you use for your products and services, the advantages they bring and any competitive edge it creates. How do you anticipate this evolving over time? Is this something you own, license or is widely available?

Intellectual Property

Intellectual property (IP) refers to creations of the mind, and includes: inventions, literary and artistic works, symbols, names, images, and designs used in commerce.

IP can be divided into two categories: Industrial property, which includes inventions (patents), trademarks, industrial designs, trade secrets and customer lists, etc;

and Copyright, which includes literary and artistic works such as novels, poems and plays, films, musical works, artistic works such as drawings, paintings, photographs and sculptures, and architectural designs. Rights related to copyright include those of performing artists in their performances, producers of phonograms in their recordings, and those of broadcasters in their radio and television programs.

If you have something unique, which you invented, your intellectual property needs to be properly protected by patents in the countries you wish to sell it. In fact, in some industries, such as the pharmaceutical world, IT, medical devices, and others, it is essential the patents are in place to protect you and the company from other companies copying and selling your invention.

Freedom to Operate and Licensing

Just as important, and often over looked with complex products, is the need to include a freedom to operate analysis. This can be an expensive undertaking, but if you are looking for a significant investment, it is likely you will have to provide this as part of the diligence process. It essentially ensures that you can market your product without infringing existing patents or patent applications under consideration. It is not the end of the world if there are patents that you may infringe, as you can always try to obtain a license from the patent owner. It is, however, best to obtain this license before moving forward with your plans as ultimately, this patent could block you from marketing your product. Also, the longer you leave it to obtain a license, the more chance the price will increase as the owner of the patent sees that you really need the license to progress.

Trade Secrets, etc.

You should not overlook other company advantages, such as, trade secrets and customer lists, which are highly valuable, and although not protectable with intellectual property rights, they should be carefully guarded and included in any valuation of a business.

If you are in a service business that creates unique reports as part of its business, then be sure to Copyright protect your documents to ensure others cannot just copy and use the materials without your permission or paying a fee.

Make sure you have addressed all the questions in this section before you move on to the next section, Market Research.

4. MARKET RESEARCH AND ANALYSIS

KEY CONTENT	ANALYSIS
Customers	Who and where are your customers that will buy the product or service? What are their key demographics? What is the basis of their purchase decision: price, quality, service, personal contact or some other factor? How will they evolve over time, or not? Generating a spreadsheet can be very helpful. It can include your customer's details: their contact details, buying habits, sales history and projected sales, along with a list of potential new customers?
Market Size	Define the potential market in unit numbers and $ value, geographic area, along with any seasonal fluctuations, and growth rates. Discuss the impact of industry trends, economic trends, government regulations, population changes and new technologies. Describe the expected annual sales of the market and over the next 3-5 years. Define all of your assumptions.
Competition	Define your key competitors, their products and services, their strengths and weaknesses and their likely strategies and response to your product or service. Describe the advantages and disadvantages of these products or services and why they are or are NOT meeting customer needs.
Market Share and Sales	Summarize what it is about your product that makes it stand out and saleable in light of the current and anticipated competitors. Define any current customers and why they have made commitments to purchase. Discuss which customers might be

	major purchasers and why. Based on your assessment of the market size and growth, and in light of your products' advantages over the competition, estimate your share of the market and the number of sales in units and dollars you will achieve over the next 3-5 years. Clearly state all your assumptions.

Quantify

Where possible it is best to quantify your market: its size in terms of customers, growth, and in value ($) based on the products purchased. It is then possible with an understanding of market share to see how your competition is performing compared to your products. Finding out why a particular competitive product attains a certain market share is more difficult as it requires you to understand your customer's motivations and needs and why they believe a particular product meets those needs.

Market research

Without market research, even in its simplest form, you cannot understand what it is your customers want and why they choose one product over another. You can start by just asking your existing customers why they buy your product and why they do not buy alternate products?

If you are a part of a large company, you can often buy market research "off the shelf" to give you the latest data on the market, but you cannot beat finding out yourself and asking the questions you want answering. Getting to know and really understand your customers needs is the basis of all good businesses.

Learning to listen and adapting your products and services to really provide the customer with a great experience can enhance your business and the bottom line. So ask your customers questions and ask your competitor's customers questions too. Not just what they like about your product, but what they don't like; and why? What would they like to have? What would really improve their experience?

The Market

Just what is your market or market segment, what products or customers define it? Is it growing? Time for a spreadsheet! It can be very useful to draw up a spreadsheet showing units sold, pricing and $ value for a market, which can form the basis of your business financial model. Are there seasonal fluctuations, geographic hotspots, is the market growing, and if so, where and why? What factors are influencing your market today: what are the industry trends, economic trends, and what is the impact of government regulations and technology trends? What do you anticipate will happen over the next several years to the market and why? Again, you can use this to create a forecast for your product.

Competition

Who are your prime competitors? Define their products or services and how they differ from yours? What are their sales history and market share? What are their strengths and weaknesses, and their current business strategies? How do they respond to your product, or how might they respond to your new initiatives? How does your product or service compare in terms of advantages and disadvantages? Are they meeting the customers' needs? How might you take business away from them? How can you differentiate your products and business from the other competitors?

Sales Projection

What is it that makes your product or service standout from the competition? What sales can you achieve? You can start to answer this by thinking about your current customers and what commitments they have made to purchase your product. You can then think about what market share you might be able to take from your competition based on your knowledge of what your competitor's customers want or need? Back to the spreadsheet: project the number of units of your products you will sell over the next time period, add in your average selling price and calculate your sales. Business plans trying to raise money need to project on average 3-5 years out and it is traditional to provide the first year sales by month.

This section is a lot of work and requires you to gather a lot of data and to make sense of it. You should complete your market research before you move onto the Marketing Plan section.

5. MARKETING PLAN

KEY CONTENT	ANALYSIS
Overall Marketing Strategy	Define your overall strategy to achieve your sales: the type of customer segments you will focus on, how you will reach them with an initial promotional push and subsequent targeted sales efforts.
Marketing Goals	Describe your top 4-6 goals for your marketing plan: one should include your overarching first 6 months sales target in units and $, and others should be objectively measurable with a clear timeline.
Positioning	Describe the value your product creates for customers, the advantage it has over the competition, and how you will create a desire in customers to purchase your product?
Pricing	The price needs to be set at the right level to allow you to penetrate the market, maintain and grow its position and make a profit. Make sure the value you bring is reflected in the price when you compare to the competition.
Advertising and Promotions	Describe the approaches you plan to take to bring your product or service to the attention of your prospective customers. Create a schedule and cost of advertising and promotion. You may want to consider traditional approaches, but also social media?
Sales and Distribution	Describe how you intend to sell and distribute the product or service. Will you employ your own sales team; use independent sales representatives, or distributors? Discuss the margins to be given to retailers, wholesalers and salesmen and compare to the competition.

The Marketing Plan Role

A marketing plan is essential for any product to help you define how you will position your product in the market place to make it as attractive as possible to your potential customers, how it will stand out from your competition and ensure that you are getting your message to those that are interested or can influence a purchase, and to ensure your product is available where and when it is needed.

The marketing plan starts with the overall marketing strategy, which should be derived from your overall company strategy and strategic imperatives (see section 2). The overarching marketing strategy should set out broad marketing objectives, which can be focused down into specific marketing goals.

Goals

What specific goals do you have for your product(s)? You might think in terms of revenue to be achieved within a certain time, or number of units sold over a period of time? Some companies focus on the number of new customers or repeat sales to existing customers? Others focus on market share, profitability, margins, sales per customer, expanding into new geographies and any number of other goals that make sense for their business and are in line with their strategic plan and strategic imperatives. The more specific you can be by using numbers and time frames, and the more measurable a goal is, the more likely you will be successful. Poorly defined goals produce poor results. Well-defined goals that are easily measured produce well-defined results.

Positioning

Defining your product so it is appealing to customers is a critical part of marketing. A positioning statement essentially defines the value your product creates for customers, why they should choose your product over the competition and the features and benefits associated with the product. The value proposition is part of this, as is your sustainable competitive advantage (see section 3). These key statements should be used throughout your advertising and promotional campaign.

Pricing

Remember, the price of your product needs to be set at the right level to allow you to penetrate the market, maintain and grow its position and make a profit. You can use comparative products as a guideline. If you offer more value in the eyes of your customer than a competitor, but charge the same price, you should be able to take market share; you may even be able to charge a higher price to reflect your added value. It is important to make sure your product's value is reflected in the price. If you set your price too low, you may be giving money away and devaluing your product in your customer's eyes. Be careful on a low price strategy too: make sure you can cover all your costs, and still make a profit or you will soon be out of business.

Advertising and Promotions

This is really the nuts and bolts of your marketing plan. What is it you are actually going to do? Advertise in the newspaper, hand out leaflets, send out an email advertisement, contact your friends, run advertisements on the radio or TV, or adverts on LinkedIn and Google, cold calling or referrals, visiting exhibitions or making public presentations? Just how will you get the word out about your product or service?

A good way to start thinking about this is to closely observe your customers. Where do they normally obtain their information about the type of product you are offering? This is where you need to put your efforts. Make sure your advertising and promotion tactics line up with your strategic and marketing goals. Make sure you cost out all the activities you plan and add it into your budget. And, most importantly, make sure you measure the impact of each of these activities as best you can, so you can make decisions which to continue with and which should be dropped in the future.

Sales and Distribution

Having created a demand for your product with your advertising and promotion campaigns, how can you make sure your customers receive their products where and when they want it. Clearly your sales activities can be part of your advertising and promotion activities, but having sold your product, it is important the customer can have access to it. You need to think about where your product needs to be, in what quantity and when it needs to be available? Will you use distributors, wholesalers or salesmen? How much will you pay them? This can be a significant part of your budget. Distribution can be very complex or very simple; very cheap or very expensive. It is an important part of your business, so think it through carefully.

Measurement

Finally, make sure you measure the effects of each of your marketing programs both in terms of the cost and the outcomes you set as goals. Did it achieve the objective you wanted? If yes, maybe repeat it or invest further? If not, perhaps it is time to stop that activity and spend your money elsewhere to better effect?

A more detailed look at how to construct a marketing plan that will truly advance your business is covered in my book, The Marketing Plan Guide.

If you are satisfied that you have the Marketing Plan section complete, it is time to think about your new and developing products in the next section: Development Plan.

6. DEVELOPMENT PLAN

KEY CONTENT	ANALYSIS
Development Plan	Describe the product development plan for existing and new products. Define the key steps, risks, and probability of success.
Milestones and Budget	Create a timeline of key milestones and the budget required to support the development and eventual launch of each product.

Product Development

The development plan is a critical part of most business plans to demonstrate what and when new products can be expected to reach the market place. The plan should include new products and any existing products, which are being updated or changed. It is important to highlight the major milestones that have to be achieved, the risk associated with each, and the cost and time it will take to complete each milestone.

The plan needs to be as realistic as possible, with timelines that make sense and costs derived from accurately projecting the work involved or detailed quotes obtained from outside vendors.

Timelines, Costs, & Risks

It is essential each key activity or step have a timeline with a start and finish date, cost, and risk assessment together with how it relates to the other activities and the overall development of the final product or service.

Development Financials

The development plan obviously ties into the marketing and distribution plan in terms of timing, cost and the likely product attributes you plan for your product or service. It should also be factored into your budget as a cost. Many companies opt to prepare separate financial projections for their development activities showing what type of revenue, profit and cash flow a new product or products can create for the company, but also to make sure the product can stand on its own as a profit making activity. Whatever you choose to do, the cost of the development activity needs to be included as a cost of your business.

Make sure you have completed this section before moving onto the next sections. For example, you will need to have all your development costs and timing ready before you can think about manufacturing and operations, and the financial plan.

7. OPERATING PLAN

KEY CONTENT	ANALYSIS
Location, Facilities & Improvements	Define the location of the business and the availability of labor, pay rates, proximity to customer and suppliers, access to wholesalers, distributors and transportation, state and local taxes, laws and regulations. Define planned facilities, changes, improvements needed as the business grows. Explain equipment required, costs and acquisition dates.
Strategy and Manufacturing Plan	Describe the process involved in the production of your product and service. Prepare a plan of costs vs. volume of sales with a breakdown of material, labor, purchased components and overheads. If manufacturing is involved, describe how quality is assured, controlled, inspected for, and what production controls and inventory controls are used. Describe the quality controls and inspection to minimize service problems and ensure customer satisfaction,
Labor Force	Exclusive of the management team, describe the local labor force, skills and education needs for the company and does the quantity and quality of personnel exist locally or in easy access? What training programs may be necessary to ensure labor performs optimally?
Distribution	Describe how products and services will be delivered, cost and systems required, and the inventory necessary to fill the pipeline.

Facilities

Where do you plan to run your business: Your home, an office, a factory or any other facility? Make sure you consider such factors as the proximity of your customers and suppliers, the availability of labor, pay rates, access to wholesalers, distributors and transportation, state and local taxes, laws and regulations, rents and upkeep of the facility. If it is an office then there is the cost of office facility or rent, the utilities, the furniture and supplies, phone, computers and Internet connection.

Try to plan what you will need from your facilities in terms of space and function, not just for today but for the next year or two so you do not have to keep moving. What changes or improvements might you need to make as the business grows? What equipment do you need; where will it go; what are the costs and acquisition dates; and what is the cost of maintaining the equipment and the facility? Don't forget the utilities!

Manufacturing Plan

The manufacturing plan for your product should be driven by the sales projection for the company, but first you should have a very clear idea of the production process, the materials required and the time and costs involved to make your product. Once you have a clear idea of the process, the materials, the costs and time associated with making your product, you can now create a manufacturing plan.

The plan, simply, starts with an estimate of the number of product units you need over time. You can then calculate how many units you need to produce each month to ensure that you have enough inventory and time to distribute the product to the point of sale in sufficient quantities. You can then add in the costs associated with making the product. It is usual to breakdown the costs to include: material, labor, purchased components and overheads. You should also include a cost to ensure quality, both quality assurance activities and quality control testing and release of your product. Don't forget to think about the production controls and inventory controls that may be needed too.

Labor

What if any, labor will you need to make, test, and sell your products? What level of education and skills are needed for each job and does the quantity and quality of persons required exist locally or are within easy commuting access. What training programs may be necessary to ensure labor performs optimally?

Distribution

How do you intend to deliver your products to your customers? Will you use a distributor, wholesaler, a retail outlet, a product carrying sales force or direct delivery by hand, by mail or by truck? What systems need to be put in place to make sure the distribution system operates efficiently and in a timely fashion? What are the costs involved and how will this affect the inventory necessary to fill the pipeline?

There is a lot to think about in this section, and it is important you complete it before moving onto the next section.

8. KEY PERSONNEL

KEY CONTENT	ANALYSIS
Organization	Define key management roles and individuals who will fill each slot. Discuss the skills that complement each other to result in an effective management team.
Key Personnel	Define duties and responsibilities of key members of management team, e.g. CEO, CFO and Senior VP level staff. Briefly describe the background and experience of each member of the team.
Management Compensation and Ownership	Define salary levels for management, benefits provided, any stock ownership and any performance related bonus schemes.
Board of Directors	Define your philosophy of the board composition and size. Identify proposed Board Members and give a brief description of their background.

Organization and Key Personnel

It is important to have a sense of the organization you need to run your business effectively and efficiently. What types of roles are required and who might be a candidate for each of those positions? Making sure the leadership team of the company is carefully picked is essential. You need people who are experts at what you need, with the right experience, a great track record of getting things done, who are trustworthy, honest, and who buy into the vision for the company. A list of your key people, their qualifications and past relevant experience and successes should be included in the business plan.

Compensation

It is usual to list out the key personnel, their salary and benefits together with their stock ownership and any stock options they have been issued. Performance related bonuses should also be noted.

Board of Directors

It is typical to also list the board members, their membership of specific committees, traditionally Human Resource, Audit, and Finance Committees, their background expertise and experience.

Some business plans include the name of their law firm, their accountants and any special advisors to the board or CEO as well.

Once you have completed this section and all the other previous sections, except the Executive Summary, you are ready to move on to the Financial Plan and Contingencies section.

9. FINANCIAL PLAN AND CONTINGENCIES

KEY CONTENT	ANALYSIS
Sources and Uses of Funds	Define funds provided by owners, any investor equity and loans provided or planned. Describe planned uses of funds for buildings, facilities, equipment, promotions, inventory, development, product launches, etc.
Financial Statements	Provide a 3 year history of the key financial statements (preferably audited): Profit and Loss Statement Cash Flow Statement Balance Sheet
Profit and Loss Forecast	Provide a 3-5 year profit and loss forecast (pro forma) by estimating your sales and returns, cost of goods, R&D costs, general and administrative costs and the resulting net income before and after taxes.
Pro Forma Cash Flow Analysis	Prepare a month by month cash flow from operations by estimating the timing of cash receipts, and disbursements such as salaries and pay, office supplies, promotional costs, equipment purchases, taxes. If cash is generated from investments or financing, this should also be added.
Pro Forma Balance Sheets	Prepare an annual balance sheet including assets (cash, inventory, accounts receivable, fixed assets - land, building, equipment), liabilities (loans, accounts payable, long term debt) and equity (share ownership, and retained earnings).
Exit Strategies and Return on Investment	Most investors will want to know how they will get their investment out, the approximate timing and the

	potential return on that investment. Exit strategies include selling the stock, going public if you are a private company, or selling the company for cash or stock in a public enterprise. The return on investment requires a calculation of value, which can be based on market comparisons or a discounted cash flow analysis.
Contingency Plans	Define key assumptions made in the business: new customer acquisition, pricing, sales, costs, and the type of variability that may occur. Also, define a few "unexpected catastrophes'" such as the competition dropping its price or introducing an identical product, etc. Now define what impact that may have and how you would react.

This is a critical section to the business plan, which most savvy investors will scrutinize very carefully. You need to define, through financial statements, how your company has performed historically and how you intend it to perform going forward.

Ownership

It is traditional to provide a capitalization table, or ownership table, which lays out the ownership structure of the company by providing a list of the owners of the company and the number of shares they own of the different classes of stock that may comprise the company.

Source and Use of Funds

This section provides a brief history of the funds invested in the business to date, their source, and what they were used to purchase in the form of the key assets of the company, and in supporting the running of the company over its history.

You should also discuss the funds you are seeking from any new investments you anticipate, and how you intend to use these funds to develop and grow your business.

Don't forget to refer to the development, marketing and operation plans you have already discussed.

A quick note to any money seeker: make sure you are asking for enough funds to take you past your next major milestone, so that if you need another investment, you have good news and time to raise it!

Financial Statements

A three year history of financial statements should be included; preferably statements that have been audited by independent auditors. It should include a profit and loss statement, a cash flow statement and a balance sheet showing data from the last three financial years. Be prepared to answer questions about your performance during this time and the impact of any key decisions you made. Your financial performance will be used as a predictor of what you might achieve in the future, so be ready to explain your future forecasts in light of your past performance.

Pro Forma Financial Statements

The pro forma statements should include financial projections for the next 3 to 5 years. The profit and loss statement should clearly show the projected sales, cost of goods, gross margin, key expenses such as research and development cost, sales and marketing expenses, general and administrative expenses, operating profits, predicted taxes and net income.

The cash flow statement should show cash from operations, cash from investing, and cash from financing. The cash flow from operations includes all the cash received from customers minus all the expenditures; don't forget that an increase in accounts receivables needs to be deducted, as it has not been received, and that an increase in inventory and any purchases made have to be added to the expenditures. Cash from investments includes purchasing and the sale of marketable securities, any loans made or collected and any plant asset purchases or sales. The cash from financing includes any proceeds from loans or stock sales, and any payments of debts.

The balance sheet essentially shows the total assets of the

company, offset by the liabilities and equity ownership. The total assets are made up of current assets (cash + marketable securities + accounts receivable + inventories), and plant and equipment. Liabilities are made up of current liabilities (accounts receivable and short term loans) and long-term debt. Stockholders equity is made up of capital stock and retained earnings.

The financial pro formas will be covered in detail in a future publication in the Fast-Track Business Expert Series.

Exit Strategies and Valuation

If the business plan is being used to obtain investments, it is important to describe the potential exit strategies for the investor. Exit strategies essentially mean the ability to liquidate (turn into cash) their position in the company. If you are a public owned company, the investor can simply sell their stock in the open market. For private companies, the exit strategies are more limited. They include, selling the investors stock to other shareholders, the company filing for an initial public offering (IPO) where investors can sell their stock in the public markets after some predefined holding period, or the acquisition of the company by a third party who pays in cash or tradable securities.

Valuation of the company at a point in the future can be estimated by using several different methods. A commonly used valuation method is by comparison to the value of similar size companies (similar revenue and profits to those predicted in your plan) in the same industry. This is relatively easy if there are public companies that resemble your company, as their financial data is readily available. However, if the only comparisons are private companies, then data for comparisons is harder to find.

A second method is known as discounted cash flow analysis. This method estimates the present value of future free cash flows of the company. To create a discounted cash flow model, you have to construct a financial model of how the company will evolve, forecasting sales, costs, equipment needed, staff levels, investments and other factors so that one can calculate how much cash the company will have in the future. Free cash flow is essentially the cash you are left with after paying out for the products or services you create. Free cash flow is equal to the net earnings – tax + depreciation – change in working capital (current assets – current liabilities) – capital expenditures. By applying a discount value one can calculate a present value of the cash flows, and a value of the company.

A third method involves using previous valuations of private investments made in the company. It is usual to assess all three of these techniques to come up with a fair market value. With an understanding of the potential future value of the company it is then relatively easy to calculate the exit value for the investor when their ownership is liquidated.

Contingency Plans

As part of your contingency planning it is a good idea to define all the key assumptions you have made in the business plan, including the rate of new customer acquisition, pricing, sales forecasts, costs and other variables in the business. It is then worth estimating what will happen to your revenues, profits and cash positions, if these key variables increase or decrease. It is also important to define a few "unexpected catastrophes" such as the competition dropping its price or introducing an identical product, etc., and then to define the impact on your financials and what you might do to counter these changes.

This activity will provide you and your investors with an assurance that you have considered that all may not play out as you planned, and that you have given some thought to how you would respond to such challenges. I would suggest including a few examples in your business plan to show you have thought about this, but to also hold some in reserve to answer questions that will surely come your way.

Almost Finished

That's it. You have almost finished your business plan. It is time to write your executive summary, which should be ideally one page or two at the most, and don't be afraid to be creative. Your executive summary is the most important part of your business plan as it should be designed to capture the imagination of the investor to make them want to learn more. I provide an example format for an Executive Summary on the next page to give you at least one possible approach.

How Long Should My Business Plan Be?

10-20 pages for a Business Plan should be fine; over 30 pages is starting to get too long.

Help? Where Can I Get Help To Write My Business Plan?

Don't panic. Help is at hand. Please contact Mark Philip at MP Consulting Services either by phone at (1-617-538-7896) or by email at mpconsultingservice@yahoo.com. For one hour of free help, contact Mark and use the code: BPG135.

EXECUTIVE SUMMARY EXAMPLE

NEWCO, Inc
123, Main Street,
www.newco.com
Notown, VX, 98765

Tel: 1-800-000-XXXX
Web:

Email: Info@Newco.com

Key Milestones
- Complete preclinical research Yr1 Q2
- Initiate Pivotal Study Yr 1
- Gain Approval Yr3
- Launch Product Yr 3
- $50M Sales Yr 4
- $300M Yr 6

Management Team
CEO: S. Anyone, MBA
CFO: U. Count, CPA
COO: M. Beaker

Advisory Team
I.M. Expert

Board
S. Anyone, MBA
A. Someone, PhD
I. Knowitall, PhD, MBA

Target Markets
USA, Europe, Japan

Funding
Require $50M

Use of Funds
Phase 3 pivotal study
Manufacturing unit

Contact
CEO: S. Anyone, MBA
Tel: 1-800-000-XXXX
Email:sanyone@newco.com

The Problem
Patients with Duchenne Muscular Dystrophy present at an early age, are in wheelchairs by their teens and die by age 30. There are no treatments.

The Solution
Replacement therapy: replace the abnormal protein, dystrophin, with a normally acting protein.

The Opportunity
US market: $XXXM; Global market: $YYYM

The Competitive Advantage
First to market opportunity, with orphan drug protection for 7 years.

The Development Plan
Normal protein showed promising disease modifying results in Phase 2 clinical trials; in the market within 4 years.

The Marketing Strategies
Launch in the USA first, then EU, then Japan. Forge strong bonds with patient groups. Start marketing 1 year prior to launch

The Team
CEO: S. Anyone, MBA. Ran several multi billion companies
CFO: U. Count, CPA. Ex Large Pharma CFO.
COO: M. Beaker. Experienced drug developer.

The Financial Projections

Financials $ (000's)	2010	2011	2012	2013	2014	2015
Revenues						
Expenditures						
Net Profit						
Net Cash						

The Investment
$XXM in three tranches: $YY0M now; $ZZM at Regulatory Filing; $AAM on approval for BB% ownership. Sell NewCo in 3 years for 5-10x return

CLOSING MATTERS.

ABOUT THE AUTHOR: MARK A. PHILIP

Mark Philip has over 20 years experience in managing businesses, both small and large, primarily in the pharmaceutical, biotechnology and medical device industry. With expertise in strategic planning, operations, product development, sales and marketing, business development, Mark has orchestrated multiple turnarounds, built product pipelines, launched new products, sold companies and created significant shareholder value.

After holding a succession of senior executive positions in biotechnology, pharmaceutical and medical device companies in Europe, the USA and Asia, Mark has also provided consulting services to a number of companies from a broad array of business sectors.

After seeing the need for professional people in many different business environments to better understand basic business principles, Mark Philip has prepared a series of course materials to help Business Executives succeed in any business setting. From his coaching of many executives in both large and small companies, Mark has created the *Fast-Track Business Expert Series ™* - a range of books and courses detailing the core skills and strategies that will help you acquire expert business experience in just a few hours.

Mark has a bachelor's degree in Applied Biology and a PhD in Stem Cell Research from Nottingham Trent University (formerly Trent Polytechnic) in the UK. After becoming The Leukemia Research Fund Postdoctoral Research Fellow at Nottingham University, Mark completed an MBA in marketing and strategy at the Lake Forest Graduate School of Management in Chicago, USA and an Advanced Leadership Course at Harvard University.

THE FAST-TRACK BUSINESS EXPERTISE SERIES ™ OF BOOKS AND COURSES.

After seeing the need for professional people in many different business environments to better understand basic business principles, Mark Philip has prepared a series of course materials to help Business Executives succeed in any business setting. From his coaching of many executives in both large and small companies, Mark has created the *Fast-Track Business Expert Series ™* - a range of books and courses detailing the core skills and strategies that will help you acquire expert business experience in just a few hours.

COURSE SERIES

- **The Strategic Plan Guide**
  Available on Amazon and CreateSpace
- **The Business Plan Guide**
  Available on Amazon and CreateSpace
- **The Marketing Plan Guide**
  In print
- **The Public Relations Plan Guide**
- **The Social Media Primer**
- **The Time Management Guide**
- **The Business Continuity Guide**
- **The Negotiations Guide**
- **The Effective Business Meetings Guide**
- **The Due Diligence Guide**
- **The Finding Your Ideal Job Guide**

MP CONSULTING SERVICES

MP Consulting Services specializes in the areas of strategic planning, leadership, marketing and social media. Mark Philip, principal at MPCS, has over 20 years experience in managing businesses, both small and large, has orchestrated multiple turnarounds, built product pipelines, launched new products, sold companies and created significant shareholder value. Let me know how I can help you with your business challenge, or help train your organization to deal with today's competitive business challenges.

Services offered across a broad range of industries, include:

- Strategic planning and strategic plan development.
- Business plans for public and private companies.
- Operational assessments and decision-making.
- Product development, program management and porfolio review.
- Sales management, support and sales efficiency.
- Marketing: market research, marketing plans, brand management and product positioning, competitive analysis, pricing models, advertising and promotion, distribution, and implementation plans.
- Public and investor relations planning.
- Social media marketing: SMM strategic planning, infrastructure, listening mechanisms, connectivity, SEO, competitive analysis, social branding, social communication, social advertising and public relations.
- Business development, assessment and transactions.
- Financing and financial projections, business models.
- Valuations and due diligence assessments.
- Support for Start Up and Entrepreneurial Ventures.

FREE GUIDES AVAILABLE FROM MP CONSULTING SERVICES

GUIDES

- **Strategic Planning Guide.**
- **Business Plan Guide.**
- **Marketing Plan Guide.**
- **Public Relations Plan Guide.**
- **Social Media Primer.**
- **Time Management Guide.**
- **Business Continuity Guide.**
- **Negotiations Guide.**
- **Effective Business Meetings Guide.**
- **Due Diligence Guide.**
- **Blog Series.**

To read more from Mark Philip, please subscribe to his blog, which can be found at:
http://mpconsulting.wordpress.com

FOR MORE INFORMATION:

For questions, more information, or help, please visit the Mark Philip Consulting Services blog at
http://mpconsulting.wordpress.com
or visit my LinkedIn account at
http://www.linkedin.com/in/markpconsulting

www.ingramcontent.com/pod-product-compliance
Lightning Source LLC
Chambersburg PA
CBHW071646170526
45166CB00003B/1450